In Joy
and
In Sorrow

In Joy
and
In Sorrow

Collected
by
Candida Lund

THE THOMAS MORE PRESS
Chicago, Illinois

ISBN 0-88347-167-1

ACKNOWLEDGEMENTS

The compiler and publisher wish to thank the following for permission to reprint excerpts from the works listed below:

George Allen & Unwin Ltd.: Selections by Eknath, Giridhar, Nanak, and Tukaram from SONGS FROM PRISON, Translations of Indian Lyrics Made in Jail by M. K. Gandhi, Adapted for the Press by John S. Hoyland, 1934. Reprinted with permission of George Allen & Unwin Ltd.

Andrews and McMeel, Inc.: "Reasoning With God About A Lake Michigan Storm" from WOMEN I'VE MET by Andrew M. Greeley. Copyright, 1979, Andrew M. Greeley. Reprinted with permission of Andrews and McMeel, Inc. All rights reserved. From PRAYERS by Michel Quoist, translated by Agnes M. Forsyth and Anne Marie de Commaille. Copyright, 1963, Sheed and Ward, Inc. Reprinted with permission of Andrews

Contents

For Maggie *et al.*

FOREWORD

MOST of us find strength and satisfaction in prayer. Some, like Mimi, Puccini's appealing heroine in *La Bohème*, "don't always go to church, but often speak to God." For others a church or temple is conducive to prayer.

"Speaking to God" is another way of defining prayer and the expression connotes as well an informality and ease, even a naturalness. With such qualities present there is less danger that prayer will become a stilted exercise. Conversation with friends, at its finest levels, is one of life's most stimulating activities.

Conversation with God can be even more exhilarating and should be as natural for us as conversation with people we value. Some will object that God does not talk back. Certainly he does not enter into the conversation in the traditional manner, but he participates in his unique way.

Frequency of prayer is what makes it part of the fabric of our lives. Prayer is not meant to be extraneous to daily living but an integral part. *In Joy and in Sorrow* was chosen as the title of this collection because I hoped that it would indicate that this was a volume reflecting the pattern of life. All of us hope that our lives will have more happiness than trials, but few are so naive as not to expect sorrows. The prayers in this book intentionally are not sharply divided between prayers of joy and those of sorrow because life is not divided that way, and some prayers reflect both moods.

21

We speak to God in two ways: in our own words and in the words of others. Obviously, both have merit. The help that we can obtain from the memorable prayers of others is the reason for this volume.

The men and women whose words will be found here have come from many walks of life. You will find poets, saints, pilots, humorists, scientists, novelists, parents, statesmen, dramatists, monks, nuns, philosophers, engineers, church leaders. Their times span the centuries from before Christ—Socrates and the Psalmist—to the present—Stevie Smith, Ogden Nash, Mother Teresa. They reflect different expressions of faiths. And the places from which they come vary significantly—from countries of Europe, Asia, North America, South America.

Such catholicity shows the common human experience, and points up the yearnings of the human spirit—for prayer in particular—no matter the role, the time, the country.

In our own day, however, the need for prayer has often been obscured. For some it may be an untried (even unheard of) experience. We live in an age of "how to" as can be inferred from the "How to . . ." books on any best seller list. Yet rarely do we ponder "how to" pray.

Having stated that, let me make clear immediately that this is not meant to be such a book. It is hoped, however, that it will make available to contemporaries prayers that have helped others in speaking to God.

A few years ago I edited an anthology called *The Days and the Nights: Prayers for Today's Woman.* Several male readers took me to task for being so restrictive. Perhaps this book will remedy that earlier restrictiveness, and show that I recognize that men, too, pray.

Rosary College   Candida Lund
River Forest, IL   Autumn, 1984

IN JOY AND IN SORROW

O God, full of surprises,
deepen our wisdom that we accept life
when it comes in paradoxes, like . . .
    sun and rain,
      storm and calm,
        pain and joy,
          defeat and victory,
            and life and death.
So keep us able when life wears many faces. Amen.

Richard Wong
(1914-   )

* * *

GOD'S WORLD

O world, I cannot hold thee close enough!
   Thy winds, thy wide grey skies!
   Thy mists, that roll and rise!
Thy woods, this autumn day, that ache and sag
And all but cry with colour! That gaunt crag
To crush! To lift the lean of that black bluff!
World, World, I cannot get thee close enough!

Long have I known a glory in it all,
     But never knew I this:
     Here such a passion is
As stretcheth me apart,—Lord, I do fear
Thou'st made the world too beautiful this year;
My soul is all but out of me,—let fall
No burning leaf; prithee, let no bird call.

             Edna St. Vincent Millay
             (1892-1950)

* * *

FOR YOUNG PERSONS

God our Father, you see your children growing up in an
unsteady and confusing world: Show them that your
ways give more life than the ways of the world, and that
following you is better than chasing after selfish goals.
Help them to take failure, not as a measure of their
worth, but as a chance for a new start. Give them
strength to hold their faith in you, and to keep alive
their joy in your creation; through Jesus Christ our
Lord, *Amen.*

The Book of Common Prayer

* * *

PRAYER FOR PEACE

Lead me from death to life,
    from falsehood to truth;
Lead me from despair to hope,
    from fear to trust;
Lead me from hate to love,
    from war to peace;
Let peace fill our heart, our world,
    our universe.

Satish Kumar

* * *

GOD OF MY LIFE

I should like to speak with You, my God, and yet what else can I speak of but You? Indeed, could anything at all exist which had not been present with You from all eternity, which didn't have its true home and most intimate explanation in Your mind and heart? Isn't everything I ever say really a statement about You?

On the other hand, if I try, shyly and hesitantly, to speak to You about Yourself, You will still be hearing about *me*. For what could I say about You except that You are *my* God, the God of my beginning and end, God of my joy and my need, God of my life?

Of course You are endlessly more than merely the God of my life—if that's all You were, You wouldn't really be God at all. But even when I think of Your towering majesty, even when I acknowledge You as someone Who has no need of me, Who is infinitely far exalted above the lowly valleys through which I drag out the paths of my life—even then I have called You once again by the same name, God of my life.

Karl Rahner
(1904-1984)

* * *

YOUNG MIND

I have been giving thought, Lord
   —you have a minute?—to getting old.
Natural enough, as the years pass.
Do the years pass more quickly, Lord?
Whatever happened to those longer
   years we used to have?
Did you discontinue them? To speed up
   the process, sort of? To replace us faster?
Hoping for improvement in the product?
Understandable.

However, getting old. Subject for today
   —and I'm *not* talking about staying young.
Indeed not; I was young once and
   wasn't mad on it. But to continue.
Getting old, a fellow said, is all in the mind.
True. It's also inclined to get into the joints,
   the digestion, and the poor old feet.
Spectacles appear, then a second pair.
Certain powers wane. Expected; allowed for.
But the fellow's right, or nearly right.

Now, Lord. To the point.
What if the *mind* gets stiff in the joints?
   Where are you then?

What if the *mind* goes lame, needs two
   pairs of specs?
Then, it would seem, a person's got trouble.
I mean, if the mind is in charge, and
   starts taking days off; loses grip.

Where are you then?
Seems it's time for a person to shut the office.

So, Lord, please, keep me young in the mind.
Let me enjoy, Lord, let me enjoy.
If creaky I must be, and many-spectacled,
and morning-stiff and food-careful,
If trembly-handed and slow-moving and
breath-short and head-noddy,
I won't complain. Not a word.
If, with your help, dear Friend, there
will dwell in this ancient monument,
A Young Mind. Please, Lord?

David Kossoff
(1919-   )

* * *

O God, who hast bound us together in this bundle of
life, give us grace to understand how our lives depend
on the courage, the industry, the honesty and integrity
of our fellowmen; that we may be mindful of their
needs, grateful for their faithfulness, and faithful in
our responsibilities to them; through Jesus Christ
our Lord.

Reinhold Niebuhr
(1892-1971)

* * *

JACET LEO XIII

Behold the aged Lion, Lord! I am
Now come to lay me down beside the Lamb.

John Banister Tabb
(1845-1909)

* * *

I challenged and I kept the Faith,
    The bleeding path alone I trod;
It darkens. Stand about my wraith,
    And harbour me—almighty God.

Hilaire Belloc
(1870-1953)

* * *

This day, O Lord—
    give me courtesy:
    give me meekness of bearing, with decision of char-
      acter:
    give me longsuffering:
    give me charity:
    give me chastity:
    give me sincerity of speech:
    give me diligence in my allotted task.

John Baillie
(1886-1960)

* * *

FOR ANY SPEAKERS

Oh God, who in the night-quiet called
Samuel to you, call us then too
and in the day-noise call that, hearing you,
we may more plainly say the nameless name.

William Bronk
(1918-   )

* * *

I have sought Thy nearness;
With all my heart have I called Thee,
And going out to meet Thee
I found Thee coming toward me.

Yehuda Halevi
(1085-1140)

* * *

PRAISE AND PRAYER

I have been well, I have been ill,
  I have been rich and poor;
I have set my back against the wall
  And fought it by the hour;

I have been false, I have been true;
  And thoro' grief and mirth,
I have done all that man can do
  To be a man of worth;

And now, when from an unknown shore,
  I dare an unknown wave,
God, who has helped me heretofore,
  O help me wi' the lave!

Robert Louis Stevenson
(1850-1894)

* * *

A SELFISH PRAYER

"Let me wake to a morning filled with your love.
Let me rejoice and be happy.
Let me see how much you can do for me.
Let your bounty be upon me.
Make all I do succeed."

Psalm 90

That's baldly put, I must admit.
What they call a "Give me" prayer.
It's also childish and out of fashion,
reducing God to a sugar daddy.
Yet, there it is, in the Book.
And who am I to try to be nobler.
Selfishness is to be overcome.
But selfish I am.
So while it may be the least of prayers,
at least it's honest.

Sean Freeman
(1930-   )

* * *

THE ROAD AHEAD

My Lord God,
I have no idea where I am going.
I do not see the road ahead of me.
I cannot know for certain where it will end.
Nor do I really know myself,
and the fact that I think I am following
    your will does not mean that I am
    actually doing so.
But I believe that the desire to please you
    does in fact please you.
And I hope I have that desire in all that I am doing.
I hope that I will never do anything apart
    from that desire.
And I know that if I do this,
you will lead me by the right road though I
    may know nothing about it.
Therefore will I trust you always though I
    may seem to be lost and in the shadow
    of death.
I will not fear, for you are ever with me.
and you will never leave me to face my perils alone.

Thomas Merton
(1915-1968)

* * *

CHRIST OF THE EVERYWHERE

Christ of the Andes, Christ of the Everywhere.
  Great Lover of the hills, the open air,
And patient Lover of impatient men
  Who blindly strive and sin and strive again,—
Thou Living Word, larger than any creed,
  Thou Love Divine, uttered in human need,—
Oh, teach the world, warring and wandering still,
  The way to Peace, the footpath of Good Will!

Henry van Dyke
(1852-1933)

* * *

Justus quidem tu es, Domine, si disputem tecum:
  verumtamen justa loquar ad te: Quare via impiorum
  prosperatur?

THOU art indeed just, Lord, if I contend
With thee; but, sir, so what I plead is just.
Why do sinners' ways prosper? and why must
Disappointment all I endeavour end?
    Wert thou my enemy, O thou my friend,
How wouldst thou worse, I wonder, than thou dost
Defeat, thwart me? Oh, the sots and thralls of lust
Do in spare hours more thrive than I that spend,
Sir, life upon thy cause. See, banks and brakes
Now, leavèd how thick! lacèd they are again
With fretty chervil, look, and fresh wind shakes
Them; birds build—but not I build; no, but strain,
Time's eunuch, and not breed one work that wakes.
Mine, O thou lord of life, send my roots rain.

                              Gerard Manley Hopkins
                                    (1844-1889)

* * *

DEAR GOD, THE DAY IS GREY

Dear God, the day is grey. My house
is not in order. Lord, the dust
sifts through my rooms and with my fear,
I sweep mortality, outwear
my brooms, but not this leaning floor
which lasts and groans. I walking here,
still loathe the labors I would love
and hate the self I cannot move.

And God, I know the unshined boards,
the flaking ceiling, various stains
that mottle these distempered goods,
the greasy cloths, the jagged tins,
the dog that paws the garbage cans.
I know what laborings, love, and pains,
my blood would will, yet will not give:
the knot of hair that clogs the drains
clots in my throat. My dyings thrive.

The refuse, Lord, that I put out
burns in vast pits incessantly.
All piecemeal deaths, trash, undevout
and sullen sacrifice, to thee.

Anne Halley

* * *

A PRAYER

Give me work to do;
Give me health;
Give me joy in simple things.
Give me an eye for beauty,
A tongue for truth,
A heart that loves,
A mind that reasons,
A sympathy that understands;
Give me neither malice nor envy,
But a true kindness
And a noble common sense.
At the close of each day
Give me a book,
And a friend with whom
I can be silent.

                        Anonymous

* * *

WHEN WILT THOU SAVE THE PEOPLE?

When wilt Thou save the people?
O God of mercy, when?
Not kings and lords, but nations!
Not thrones and crowns, but men!
Flowers of Thy heart, O God, are they;
Let them not pass, like weeds, away—
God save the people!

                        Ebenezer Elliott
                        (1781-1849)

* * *

You have come down, Lord, into this day which is now beginning. But alas, how infinitely different in degree is your presence for one and another of us in the events which are now preparing and which all of us together will experience! In the very same circumstances which are soon to surround me and my fellow-men you may be present in small measure, in great measure, more and more or not at all.

Therefore, Lord, that no poison may harm me this day, no death destroy me, no wine befuddle me, that in every creature I may discover and sense you, I beg you: give me faith.

Pierre Teilhard de Chardin
(1881-1955)
Hymn of the Universe

* * *

Give me beauty in the inward soul; and may the inward and the outer man be at one. May I reckon wisdom to be wealth, and may I have so much gold as a temperate man and only he can bear and carry. . . . This prayer, I think, is enough for me.

Socrates
(469-399 B.C.)

* * *

A PRAYER

O Mary, fragile mother,
hear me, hear me now
although I do not know your words.
The black rosary with its silver Christ
lies unblessed in my hand
for I am the unbeliever.
Each bead is round and hard between my fingers,
a small black angel.
O Mary, permit me this grace,
this crossing over,
although I am ugly,
submerged in my own past
and my own madness.
Although there are chairs
I lie on the floor.
Only my hands are alive,
touching beads.
Word for word, I stumble.
A beginner, I feel your mouth touch mine.

Anne Sexton
(1928-1974)

* * *

MORT'S CRY

Oh, Lamb of God I am
Too sharp, too tired,
Make me more amiable, Oh Lamb,
Less tired,
No longer what I am.

So cried poor Colonel Mort, I heard him cry,
And yet he was a good man and fought energetically,
His men loved him, his country too, and did not find
   him tearful,
Then what a funny cry for him! I thought it made him
   wonderful.

Change me, Lord Lamb,
Leave me not as I am.

Stevie Smith
(1902-1971)

* * *

THE ACATHISTOS HYMN

XXIII

Exalting thy childbearing
we all glorify thee, too,
as a living temple, O mother of God,
for in thy womb dwelt he,
who holdeth all in his hand,
     the Lord.
He hallowed thee, he honoured thee,
and taught all to praise thee:

Translated by
G. G. Meersseman

* * *

YOUTH PRAYS FOR PEACE

Lord, we are the Youth of every land,
  Pleading for peace;
We are the ones who will be sacrificed
  Unless wars cease;
We are the ones elected, Lord, to pay
  A price too high.
You gave us life, and it is not Your will
  That we should die.

Open the blind eyes of our leaders, Lord,
  In every land;
Open their hearts and minds and make them wise
  To understand
That war is sad and horrible and wrong,
  And useless quite;
That we, the clean, strong Youth of earth,
  Have the good right
To life and love and happiness and peace.

We would not be
Killers of men—we want to walk the earth
  Clean-handed, free
From war with all its horrors, lust, and greed,
  Its dark despair.
Lord, may there never be another war—
  This is our prayer.

Grace Noll Crowell
(1877-1969)

* * *

Grant me that peace which dwells in garnered harvests, in things set finally in order, in folded flocks. Let me now *be*, having done with *becoming*. Weary am I of my heart's bereavements, and too old to put forth branches anew. One by one I have lost my friends and foes, and the path of melancholy pleasures that lies before me is all too clear. After long wanderings I have come back to mine own place and, when I look around me, I see all men worshipping the golden calf, not out of self-interest but out of sheer stupidity. And the young folk of today are more alien to me than young barbarians without a God. Laden am I with useless treasure, as with a music that has lost its potency for ever.

Reveal Thyself to me, O Lord; for all things are hard to one who has lost touch with God.

Antoine de Saint-Exupéry
(1900-1944)
The Wisdom of the Sands

* * *

PRAYER

If I must of my Senses lose,
I pray Thee, Lord, that I may choose
Which of the Five I shall retain
Before oblivion clouds the brain.
My Tongue is generations dead,
My Nose defiles a comely head;
For hearkening to carnal evils
My Ears have been the very devil's.
And some have held the Eye to be
The instrument of lechery,
More furtive than the Hand in low
And vicious venery—Not so!
Its rape is gentle, never more
Violent than a metaphor.
In truth, the Eye's the abettor of
The holiest platonic love:
Lip, Breast and Thigh cannot possess
So singular a blessedness.
Therefore, O Lord, let me preserve
The Sense that does so fitly serve,
Take Tongue and Ear—all else I have—
Let Light attend me to the grave!

Theodore Roethke
(1908-1963)

* * *

PRAYER FOR PAIN

I DO not pray for peace nor ease,
     Nor truce from sorrow:
No suppliant on servile knees
     Begs here against to-morrow!

Lean flame against lean flame we flash,
     O Fates that meet me fair;
Blue steel against blue steel we clash—
     Lay on, and I shall dare!

But Thou of deeps the awful Deep,
     Thou Breather in the clay,
Grant this my only prayer—Oh keep
     My soul from turning gray!

For until now, whatever wrought
     Against my sweet desires,
My days were smitten harps strung taut,
     My nights were slumberous lyres.

And howso'e'er the hard blow rang
     Upon my battered shield,
Some lark-like, soaring spirit sang
     Above my battle-field.

And through my soul of stormy night
     The zigzag blue flame ran.
I asked no odds—I fought my fight—
     Events against a man.

But now—at last—the gray mist chokes
  And numbs me. Leave me pain!
Oh, let me feel the biting strokes,
  That I may fight again!

John G. Neihardt
(1881-1973)

* * *

TEMPER MY INTEMPERANCE

Temper my intemperance, O Lord,
O hallowed, O adored,
My heart's creator, mighty, wild,
Temper Thy bewildered child.
Blaze my eye and blast my ear,
Let me never fear to fear
Nor forget what I have heard,
Even your voice, my Lord.
Even your Word.

Madeleine L'Engle
(1918-   )

* * *

GRACE BEFORE SLEEP

How can our minds and bodies be
Grateful enough that we have spent
Here in this generous room, we three,
This evening of content?
Each one of us has walked through storm
And fled the wolves along the road;
But here the hearth is wide and warm,
And for this shelter and this light
Accept, O Lord, our thanks to-night.

Sara Teasdale
(1884-1933)

* * *

REASONING WITH GOD ABOUT
A LAKE MICHIGAN STORM
(*for which He was clearly responsible*)

So, what mighty lord made you mad this time?
Banshee winds, killer waves, psychotic surf
This storm no chance, you must have me in mind
The house shakes. Quit rocking my poor turf!
I take your noise personally, of course
For waves of this absurd and foolish size
You must cause, not low pressure, natural force
Such a storm I will not demythologize.

I mean, tell me what have I done wrong?
Still the frenzy, calm yourself, postpone my fate
My verses inept may be but not too long
Let's clear this up. I promise I'll go straight
Okay, if you say so I'll wait awhile
Whatdaya mean, some angel lost my file?

Andrew M. Greeley
(1928-   )

* * *

Grant, Lord, this boon alone:

I ask not riches nor prosperity,
I ask not Heaven:

But this I ask,
Gift far beyond all other gifts,
Which is itself,
Life, bliss, salvation:

I ask this only—
Fellowship undying
With that which is supremely, wholly Good.

**Tukaram
(b. 1608)**

* * *

THE EVERLASTING MERCY

O Christ who holds the open gate,
O Christ who drives the furrow straight,
O Christ, the plough, O Christ, the laughter
Of holy white birds flying after,
Lo, all my heart's field red and torn,
And thou wilt bring the young green corn
The young green corn divinely springing,
The young green corn for ever singing;
And when the field is fresh and fair
Thy blessed feet shall glitter there,
And we will walk the weeded field
And tell the golden harvest's yield,
The corn that makes the holy bread
By which the soul of man is fed,
The holy bread, the food unpriced,
The everlasting mercy, Christ.

John Masefield
(1878-1967)

* * *

HYMN AGAINST PESTILENCE

GOD'S blessing lead us, help us!
May Mary's Son veil us!
May we be under His safeguard to-night!
Whither we go may He guard us well!

Whether in rest or motion,
Whether sitting or standing,
The Lord of Heaven against every strife,
This is the prayer that we will pray.

May the prayer of Abel son of Adam,
Enoch, Elias help us;
May they save us from swift disease
On whatever side, throughout the noisy world.

Noah and Abraham,
Isaac the wonderful son,
May they surround us against pestilence,
That famine may not come to us!

We entreat the father of three tetrads,
And Joseph their junior:
May their prayers save us
To the King many-angeled, noble!

May Moses the good leader protect us,
Who protected us through Rubrum Mare,
Joshua, Aaron Amre's son,
David the bold lad.

May Job with his trials
Protect us past the poisons!
May God's prophets defend us,
With Maccabee's seven sons!

John the Baptist we invoke,
May he be a safeguard to us, a protection!
May Jesus with His apostles
Be for our help against danger!

St. Colman
(Eighth Century)

* * *

A FAMILY GRACE

Bless our friends
Bless our food
Lord, We're gathered together.

Feel our joy
See our love
As we break bread together.

Friendship and love
Are our guiding light
Guiding light forever.

Bless our friends
Bless our food
Seeing you in each other.

The Conrad De Paul Family
(Twentieth Century)

* * *

THE KIRKUDBRIGHT GRACE

Some have meat and cannot eat,
Some cannot eat that want it:
But we have meat and we can eat,
Sae let the Lord be thankit.

Robert Burns
(1759-1796)

* * *

Lord, give me an open heart to find you everywhere, to glimpse the heaven enfolded in a bud, and experience eternity in the smallest act of love.

Mother Teresa of Calcutta
(1910-   )

* * *

GLORY TO THEE MY GOD THIS NIGHT

Teach me to live, that I may dread
The grave as little as my bed.

Bishop Thomas Ken
(1637-1711)

* * *

D'AVALOS' PRAYER

When the last sea is sailed, when the last shallow
charted,
When the last field is reaped, and the last harvest
stored,
When the last fire is out and the last guest departed,
Grant the last prayer that I shall pray, Be good to
me, O Lord!

And let me pass in a night at sea, a night of storm and
thunder,
In the loud crying of the wind through sail and rope
and spar.
Send me a ninth great peaceful wave to drown and roll
me under
To the cold tunny-fishes' home where the drowned
galleons are.

And in the dim green quiet place far out of sight and
hearing,
Grant I may hear at whiles the wash and thresh of
the sea-foam
About the fine keen bows of the stately clippers
steering
Towards the lone northern star and the fair ports
of home.

John Masefield
(1878-1967)

* * *

AN ANCIENT IRISH PRAYER

I offer thee—
Every flower that ever grew,
Every bird that ever flew,
Every wind that ever blew.
    Good God!
Every thunder rolling,
Every church bell tolling,
Every leaf and sod.
    Laudamus Te!
I offer thee—
Every wave that ever moved,
Every heart that ever loved,
Thee, thy Father's Well-Beloved.
    Dear Lord.
Every river dashing,
Every lightning flashing,
Like an angel's sword.
    Benedicamus Te.
I offer thee—
Every cloud that ever swept
O'er the skies, and broke and wept
In rain, and with the flowerets slept.
    My King!
Each communicant praying,
Every angel staying
Before thy throne to sing.
    Adoramus Te!
I offer thee—
Every flake of virgin snow,
Every spring of earth below,

Every human joy and woe,
My Love!
O Lord! And all thy glorious
Self o'er death victorious,
Throned in heaven above.
Glorificamus Te!

* * *

This is my last petition:—

My God, who knowest all,
Be very near to me:

Send down thy grace, thy love,
As here my soul, adoring,
Bows at thy feet:

This, this is all I need,
Thyself, thy grace.

Tukaram
(b. 1608)

* * *

WHO FEELS IT

Lord, my despairs strengthen as your despair;
so this gayety, these joys,
are sourceless other than as your joy.
As so. Let there be nothing, Lord, of mine.

Let all my loves be only as you
and lovers love in me the same as I.
Let nothing be the nothing still it was
always, and will, except as it be you.

And you, my lord, unable to other be,
be all only and despair absolute.
Joy, then: nothing possible
except the all: all possible: the joy!

William Bronk
(1918-   )

* * *

Creator of the bread we eat
So that our mortal lives be fed
Your loving kindness does entreat
Us to take you for daily bread.
O Bread that fell down from the Sky,
May you our hungry souls supply.

Jan and Kasper Luiken
(Seventeenth Century)

* * *

THANKSGIVING PRAYER
1981

We have seen years of death
and continents of terror
Cambodia, Iran, Afghanistan,
Lebanon, El Salvador and Laos

You gave an Earth of beauty
we foul it with pollution,
murder, assassination
You gave an Earth of plenty
but the Sahel starves
and a billion go hungry to bed

You gave us dominion over nature
we make bombs instead of bread
You gave us love
we make hate

For the gifts, O God, our thanks
but one more .... Wisdom
else we die
on the earth we raped

                              Ezra Sensibar
                              (1905-   )

* * *

HOPE

"Why so depressed, my spirit,
why do you sigh so forlornly?
Put your hope in God.
For I shall see and praise him yet,
my savior and my God."

Psalm 43

In descending order we place our hope:
In knowledge,
in skill,
in luck,
in miracles,
and when all fails
where can we turn?
To bleak despair?
And in the heart of darkness. . .
can it be?
A speck of light
that grows from nothing.
For when all is lost at last,
there is left only what was first.
Hope, our God, in you.

Sean Freeman
(1930-   )

* * *

JESU DULCIS MEMORIA

Wish us good morning when we wake
And light us, Lord, with Thy day-break.
Beat from our brains the thicky night
And fill the world up with delight.

Gerard Manley Hopkins
(1844-1889)

* * *

Now I wake and see the light
'Tis God who has kept me through the night
I lift my voice and humbly pray
That He will keep me through the day.

Anonymous

* * *

PRAYER OF LONELINESS

THIS IS THE PRAYER of loneliness.

Have pity on me, O Lord, for the burden of my solitude is more than I can bear. Nothing have I to look forward to, and no voice comes to me in this room where I sit alone. Nevertheless, it is not human presences I crave, since I feel myself even more derelict when I plunge into the crowd. Yet many another woman there is like me, alone in a house like mine, who none the less feels contented with her lot, if those whom she loves are going about their tasks elsewhere in the house. She can neither hear nor see them. For the moment she is receiving nothing from them. But in knowing that these others are in the house—unseen, unheard albeit—she finds her happiness.

O Lord, I too, ask for nothing that may be seen or heard. Thy miracles touch not the senses. If Thou willst but enlighten my spirit as to this my dwelling, surely I shall be healed of my distress.

The wanderer in the desert, if he belong to a house that is dwelt in, has joy of it, even though it lie at the world's utmost rim. No distance can prevent him from being sustained by it, and, should he die in the desert he dies in love. Therefore, O Lord, I ask not even this, that my dwelling place should be anear.

If, walking in a crowd, a man sees all of a sudden a face that thrills him, lo, he is a man transfigured, even though that face be not for him! Thus it was with the soldier who loved a queen. He became the soldier of a queen, and all his life was changed. Therefore, O Lord, I ask not even this, that the dwelling place whereof I dream be promised me.

Far out on the high seas rove fervent men who give their lives to seeking an isle existing only in their dream. Now and again they hymn, these happy mariners, that island of the blest, and their hearts swell with joy. And it is not the hoped-for landfall that crowns their cup of happiness, but the hymn they sing. Therefore O Lord, I ask not even this, that somewhere in the world there should exist the dwelling place I crave. . . .

Loneliness is bred of a mind that has grown earthbound. For the spirit has its homeland, which is the realm of the meaning of things. Thus is it with the temple, when it bespeaks the meaning of the stones. Only in this boundless empyrean can the mind take wing. Not in things in themselves does it rejoice, but only in the visage which it reads behind them and which binds them into oneness. Grant me but this, O Lord: that I may learn to read.

Then for ever will be lifted from my shoulders the burden of my solitude.

Antoine de Saint-Exupery
(1900-1944)
The Wisdom of the Sands

* * *

My boat is very small,
Heavily laden with stones:

The waves run high around,
The stream is wide, and very swift:

The tempests smite my boat,
Dark rain-clouds fill the sky:

Take thou the helm, my God,
Oh let thy mercy steer her on,
And bring her to the farther shore in peace.

Giridhar
(Seventeenth Century)

* * *

THE GRANDFATHER'S GRACE

Well, Sir, we've been getting along pretty good for quite a while now, and we're certainly much obliged. Remember, all we ask is just to go along and be happy in our own sort of way. Of course we want to keep our health, but as far as anything else is concerned, we'll leave it to You. Thank You.

Moss Hart (1904-1961)
and George S. Kaufman (1889-1961)

* * *

O all the problems other people face
we have intensifed & could not face
until at last we feel completely alone
thick in a quart of company a day.

I knew I had a problem with that stuff
& problems with my wife & child & work;
But all what help I found left me intact
safe with a quart of feral help a day.

DT's, convulsions. Hospitals galore.
Projectile vomiting hours, intravenous,
back in the nearest bar the seventh day.
God made a suggestion. I went home

and I am in the 4th week of the third treatment
& I am *hurting*, daily, & when I jerk
a few scales seem to fall away from my eyes
until with perfect clarity enough

seems to be visible to keep me sane
& sober toward the bed where I will die.
I pray that You may grant me a yielding will.

            I pray that my will may be attuned to
                Your will for & with me.

                        John Berryman
                        (1914-1972)

                * * *

HOW BEAUTIFUL IS OUR GOD!

Morning sun, evening sun,
gliding over the waters,
light bathing in the waves,
beautiful beyond words . . .
God, our Father, immerse us
in your beauty!

Fire of God, fire over the earth,
enkindling in our hearts . . .
Christ Jesus, we want to live,
to live with soul aflame!

Storm wind, gusty wind,
folly of God at the center of our lives . . .
Spirit, come from every corner
of the world,
breathe, and let the storm break forth!

Pierre Talec
(1933-   )

* * *

Heavenly Father and God of mercy,
we no longer look for Jesus among the dead,
for he is alive and has become the Lord of life.
From the waters of death you raise us with him
and renew your gift of life within us.
Increase in our minds and hearts
the risen life we share with Christ
and help us to grow as your people
toward the fullness of eternal life with you.
We ask this through Christ our Lord.
                                        Amen.

                        Liturgy of the Mass
                        Second Sunday of Easter

                        * * *

PRAYER AT THE END OF A ROPE

Dear Lord, observe this bended knee,
This visage meek and humble,
And heed this confidential plea,
Voiced in a reverent mumble.

I ask no miracles nor stunts,
No heavenly radiogram,
I only beg for once, just once,
To not be in a jam.

One little moment thy servant craves
Of being his own master;
One placid vale between the waves
Of duty and disaster.

Oh, when the postman's whistle shrills,
Just once, Lord, let me grin:
Let me have settled last month's bills
Before this month's come in.

Let me not bite more off the cob
Than I have teeth to chew;
Please let me finish just one job
Before the next is due.

Consider, too, my social life,
Sporadic though it be;
Why is it only mental strife
That pleasure brings to me?

For months, when people entertain,
Me they do not invite;
Then suddenly invitations rain,
All for the self-same night.

R.S.V.P.'s I pray thee send
Alone and not in bunches,
Or teach me I cannot attend
Two dinners or two lunches.

Let me my hostess not insult,
Not call her diamonds topaz;
Else harden me to the result
Of my fantastic faux pas.

One little lull, Lord, that's my plea,
Then loose the storm again,
Just once, this once I beg to be
Not in a jam. Amen.

Ogden Nash
(1902-1971)

* * *

A PRAYER FOR OLD AGE

GOD guard me from those thoughts men think
In the mind alone;
He that sings a lasting song
Thinks in a marrow-bone;

From all that makes a wise old man
That can be praised of all;
O what am I that I should not seem
For the song's sake a fool?

I pray—for fashion's word is out
And prayer comes round again—
That I may seem, though I die old,
A foolish, passionate man.

W. B. Yeats
(1865-1939)

* * *

ANNA'S PRAYER

God, formerly I lived near You. I put out my hand in the dark and touched You! You punished me and knew why. You enclosed me in Your forgiveness and I rested. Away from You I am worried, always hunted, never safe. I try to do right but do wrong. I want to be truthful but live in a lie. I make an effort to think clearly but move about in a confusing gloom.

God have mercy on us all. Do not turn away from our cry. If You are ashamed of Your creation and want to obliterate it, then do not destroy us in this slow way. Hurl Earth from its orbit and let it fall into the void beyond Your knowledge. Put out our light, silence our screams, and let us be annihilated in a moment.

God, free me from myself, free me from my prison, free me from life's fever.

Ingmar Bergman
(1918-   )

* * *

I thank you, my God, for having in a thousand different ways led my eyes to discover the immense simplicity of things. Little by little, through the irresistible development of those yearnings you implanted in me as a child, through the influence of gifted friends who entered my life at certain moments to bring light and strength to my mind, and through the awakenings of spirit I owe to the successive initiations, gentle and terrible, which you caused me to undergo: through all these I have been brought to the point where I can no longer see anything, nor any longer breathe, outside that *milieu* in which all is made one.

Pierre Teilhard de Chardin
(1881-1955)
Hymn of the Universe

* * *

My God,
Thou, who art mercy and love,
Ocean-deep,
Ocean-wide,
Hear this my prayer:

At one sharp cry of pain
Thou art with the despairing soul:

In pity, power, saviour-love
Thou comest:

All lovely, gracious things,
Thou teachest:

Grant this my prayer,
That evermore my soul may dwell intent
In vision of thy beauty.

                                 Eknath
                              (b. 1548)

                    * * *

Shepherd! that with Thine amorous, sylvan song
Hast broken the slumber that encompassed me,
Who mad'st Thy crook from the accursed tree,
On which Thy powerful arms were stretched so
   long!
Lead me to mercy's ever-flowing fountains:
For Thou my Shepherd, guard, and guide shalt be;
I will obey Thy voice, and wait to see
Thy feet all-beautiful upon the mountains.
Hear Shepherd! Thou who for Thy flock art dying,
Oh, wash away these scarlet sins, for Thou
Rejoicest at the contrite sinner's vow.
Oh wait! to Thee my weary soul is crying,
Wait for me! Yet why ask it, when I see.
With feet nailed to the cross, Thou'rt waiting still
   for me!

Lope de Vega
(1562-1635)
Translated by
Henry W. Longfellow
(1807-1882)

* * *

PRAYERS OF STEEL

LAY me on an anvil, O God.
Beat me and hammer me into a crowbar.
Let me pry loose old walls.
Let me lift and loosen old foundations.

Lay me on an anvil, O God.
Beat me and hammer me into a steel spike.
Drive me into the girders that hold a skyscraper to-
gether.
Take red-hot rivets and fasten me into the central
girders.
Let me be the great nail holding a skyscraper through
blue nights into white stars.

Carl Sandburg
(1878-1967)

* * *

Tonight I ask you to help me to love.

Grant me, Lord, to spread true love in the world.
Grant that by me and by your children it may penetrate
   a little into all circles, all societies, all economic and
   political systems, all laws, all contracts, all rulings;
Grant that it may penetrate into offices, factories,
   apartment buildings, movie houses, dance halls;
Grant that it may penetrate the hearts of men and that I
   may never forget that the battle for a better world is a
   battle of love, in the service of love.

Help me to love, Lord,
   not to waste my powers of love,
   to love myself less and less in order to love others
   more and more,
That around me, no one should suffer or die because I
   have stolen the love they needed to live.

Michel Quoist
(1921-   )

* * *

LATTER DAY PSALMS

Somewhere there is Grace, Lord,
Was I not told it as a child
When the sound of the sparrow
Filled my heart with delight
And the rain fell like friendship on my head.
   Now the call of the cuckoo
Cannot calm my aching heart
And my soul is tormented with fear.
   Have mercy, Lord, for I have travelled far
Yet all my knowledge is as nothing.
My days are numbered. Time titters
As I stumble down the street.

Forgiveness, O forgive me, Lord,
Close my critical eye
Take me to your breast
For how else may I die.

                              Cliff Ashby
                              (1918-   )

* * *

PRAYER AT AN IMPASSE

*"Our eyes are upon you, our God,
for we know not what to do."*

II Chronicles 20:12

Your gift of free will is a great blessing
but today I'd like to return it.
It's not often that alternatives are so equal,
or so final.
To seize any one of them is to kill the others.
And I'm not sure which is best.
Flipping coins is for the heathen.
Lord, I leave it up to you.
Help!

Sean Freeman
(1930-   )

* * *

I THANK THEE, LORD

I thank thee O Lord for my beautiful bed
Have mercy on those who have none
And may all thy children still happier lie
When they to thy kingdom come.

Stevie Smith
(1902-1971)

* * *

A CANDLE IN THE DARK

Matthew, Mark, Luke, and John,
The Bed be blest that I lie on.
Four angels to my bed,
Four angels round my head,
One to watch, and one to pray,
And two to bear my soul away.

Thomas Ady
(c. 1656)

* * *

AFTER A TRAGIC LOSS

O God, help me to live with my grief!

Death has taken my beloved, and I feel that I cannot go on. My faith is shaken; my mind keeps asking: Why? Why does joy end in sorrow? Why does love exact its price in tears? Why?

O God, help me to live with my grief!

Help me to accept the mystery of life. Help me to see that even if my questions were answered, even if I did know why, the pain would be no less, the loneliness would remain bitter beyond words. Still my heart would ache.

O God, help me to triumph over my grief!

Help me to endure this night of anguish. Help me to walk through the darkness with faith in tomorrow. Give me comfort; give me courage; turn me to deeds that bless the living.

O God, help me to triumph over my grief!

Gates of Prayer:
The New Union Prayer book

* * *

God our Father,
we rejoice in the faith that draws us together,
aware that selfishness can drive us apart.
Let your encouragement be our constant strength.
Keep us one in the love that has sealed our lives,
help us to live as one family
the gospel we profess.
                              Amen.

                    Liturgy of the Mass
            Eleventh Sunday in Ordinary Time

                        * * *

Lord, teach me the art of patience whilst I am well,
and give me the use of it when I am sick. In that day
either lighten my burden or strengthen my back. Make
me, who so often in my health have discovered my
weakness, presuming on my own strength, to be strong
in my sickness when I rely solely on thy assistance.

                              Thomas Fuller
                              (1608-1661)

                        * * *

O blessed God, O Savior sweet,
　O Jesus, look on me!
O Christ, my King, refuse me not,
　Though late I come to Thee!

I come to Thee, confounded quite
　With sorrow and with shame,
When I beheld Thy bitter wounds
　And knew I did the same.

Nicholas Postgate
(Seventeenth Century)

* * *

EVENSONG

THE embers of the day are red
Beyond the murky hill.
The kitchen smokes: the bed
In the darkling house is spread:
The great sky darkens overhead,
And the great woods are shrill.
So far have I been led,
Lord, by Thy will:
So far I have followed, Lord, and
    wondered still.

The breeze from the embalmèd land
Blows sudden toward the shore,
And claps my cottage door.
I hear the signal, Lord—I understand.
The night at Thy command
Comes. I will eat and sleep and will not
    question more.

                    Robert Louis Stevenson
                         (1850-1894)

                    * * *

FREEDOM

O God, when you created man you gave him the gift of freedom. All else that lives is bound to the laws of nature. The plant grows as it must, and the animal follows the necessity of its being; but to man you have given the mystery of inner beginning. He can act from within himself; therefore his action belongs to him, and in his action he belongs to himself. In this freedom he should have served you, but he used it to revolt against you. Thereafter it was lost, and he became a servant. But you did not abandon him to himself. You sent your Son into the world, and he announced to man a higher freedom. He calls each one of us and stretches out his hand to him that he may believe in him, trust in him, obey him and so conquer his slavery.

Romano Guardini
(1885-1968)

* * *

THE HURRICANE

LO, Lord, Thou ridest!
Lord, Lord, Thy swifting heart

Naught stayeth, naught now bideth
But's smithereened apart!

Ay! Scripture flee'th stone!
Milk-bright, Thy chisel wind

Rescindeth flesh from bone
To quivering whittlings thinned—

Swept—whistling straw! Battered,
Lord, e'en boulders now out-leap

Rock sockets, levin-lathered!
Nor, Lord, may worm out-deep

Thy drum's gambade, its plunge abscond!
Lord God, while summits crashing

Whip sea-kelp screaming on blond
Sky-seethe, high heaven dashing—

Thou ridest to the door, Lord!
Thou bidest wall nor floor, Lord!

Hart Crane
(1899-1932)

* * *

THE PRAYER ON WINIFRED HOLTBY'S GRAVE

Give me work
Till my life shall end
And life
Till my work is done.

* * *

Give me a sense of humor, Lord,
Give me the grace to see a joke,
To get some happiness from life
And pass it on to other folk.

Anonymous

* * *

NONDUM

'Verily Thou art a God that hidest Thyself.'
IS. xlv. 15.

GOD, though to Thee our psalm we raise
No answering voice comes from the skies;
To Thee the trembling sinner prays
But no forgiving voice replies;
Our prayer seems lost in desert ways,
Our hymn in the vast silence dies.

We see the glories of the earth
But not the hand that wrought them all:
Night to a myriad worlds gives birth,
Yet like a lighted empty hall
Where stands no host at door or hearth
Vacant creation's lamps appal.

We guess; we clothe Thee, unseen King,
With attributes we deem are meet;
Each in his own imagining
Sets up a shadow in Thy seat;
Yet know not how our gifts to bring,
Where seek Thee with unsandalled feet.

And still th'unbroken silence broods
While ages and while aeons run,
As erst upon chaotic floods
The Spirit hovered ere the sun
Had called the seasons' changeful moods
And life's first germs from death had won.

And still th'abysses infinite
Surround the peak from which we gaze.

Deep calls to deep and blackest night
Giddies the soul with blinding daze
That dares to cast its searching sight
On being's dread and vacant maze.

And Thou art silent, whilst Thy world
Contends about its many creeds
And hosts confront with flags unfurled,
And zeal is flushed and pity bleeds
And truth is heard, with tears impearled,
A moaning voice among the reeds.

My hand upon my lips I lay;
The breast's desponding sob I quell;
I move along life's tomb-decked way
And listen to the passing bell
Summoning men from speechless day
To death's more silent, darker spell.

Oh! till Thou givest that sense beyond,
To show Thee that Thou art, and near,
Let patience with her chastening wand
Dispel the doubt and dry the tear;
And lead me child-like by the hand;
If still in darkness not in fear.

Speak! whisper to my watching heart
One word—as when a mother speaks
Soft, when she sees her infant start,
Till dimpled joy steals o'er its cheeks.
Then, to behold Thee as Thou art,
I'll wait till morn eternal breaks.

                    Gerard Manley Hopkins
                         (1844-1889)

AUTUMN DAY

Lord, it is time. The summer was very big.
Lay thy shadow on the sundials,
and on the meadows let the winds go loose.

Command the last fruits that they shall be full;
give them another two more southerly days,
press them on to fulfillment and drive
the last sweetness into the heavy wine.

Who has no house now, will build him one no more.
Who is alone now, long will so remain,
will wake, read, write long letters
and will in the avenues to and fro
restlessly wander, when the leaves are blowing.

Rainer Maria Rilke
(1875-1926)

* * *

THE LAST PRAYER OF PETITION EVER
(*written between New York and Chicago 35,000 feet up*)

Sigmund Freud has put me wise
that God is merely the me
afraid to face the exploding crash of a 747
from the inside.

Also it is common knowledge
that doctors reserve the back wards
for thumb-sucking parental fixations
who daddy God for daily bread
and end up both hungry and bananas.

Theologians, always the last to know,
go on asking for little red wagons
when everyone knows they are delivered
by Sears & Roebuck.

So
heaven is not stormed by my "gimmes."
I no longer beg God
"to make mine enemies
the footstool under my feet."
I am busy with the upholstering myself.
My prayer life has taken a collegial,
adult, Vatican IIish turn.
I do not beseech a mercy or beg an intercession
(needless to say importuning is out)
but consult with the Senior Partner
on affairs personal, social, and cosmic.

So it is
I wonder who was addressed
when in the sudden drop of an air pocket
my heart relocated to the space behind my teeth
and someone sitting in my seat screamed,
"O my God don't let the plane fall!"

John Shea
(1941-   )

* * *

GOD OF MY PRAYER

I should like to speak with You about my prayer, O Lord. And though it often seems to me that You pay little heed to what I try to say to You in my prayers, please listen to me carefully now.

O Lord God, I don't wonder that my prayers fall so short of You—even I myself often fail to pay the least bit of attention to what I'm praying about. So often I consider my prayer as just a job I have to do, a duty to be performed. I "get it out of the way" and then relax, glad to have it behind me. When I'm at prayer, I'm at my "duty," instead of being with You.

Yes, that's my prayer. I admit it. And yet, my God, I find it hard to be sorry for praying so poorly. How can a man hope to speak with You? You are so distant and so mysterious. When I pray, it's as if my words have disappeared down some deep, dark well, from which no echo ever comes back to reassure me that they have struck the ground of Your heart.

Lord, to pray my whole life long without hearing an answer, isn't that too much to ask? You see how I run away from You time and time again, to speak with men who give me an answer, to busy myself with things that give me some kind of response. You see how much I *need* to be answered. And yet, my prayers never receive a word of reply. Or should I say that the interior motion that comes to me in prayer, the occasional light I receive in meditation, is Your word, Your enlightenment? This, of course, is the pat and ready answer which pious writers are so eager to give. But I find it very hard to believe. Again and again I find only myself in all these experiences, only the empty echo of my own cry, when it's Your word, You Yourself, that I want to hear.

Karl Rahner
(1904-1984)

* * *

Father in heaven,
the hand of your loving kindness
powerfully yet gently guides all the
    moments of our day.
Go before us in our pilgrimage of life,
anticipate our needs and prevent our
    falling.
Send your Spirit to unite us in faith,
that sharing in your service,
we may rejoice in your presence.
We ask this through Christ our Lord.
                                    Amen.

                Liturgy of the Mass
            Twenty-eighth Sunday in
                    Ordinary Time

* * *

PRAYER OF A COUNTRY PRIEST

Dear God, I give You all, willingly. But I don't know how to give, I just let them take. The best is to remain quiet. Because though I may not know how to give, You know how to take. . . . Yet I would have wished to be, once, just once, magnificently generous to You!

                        Georges Bernanos
                        (1888-1948)

* * *

O Lord my God, since the way of the Cross is the way that all in this life must walk, of what state or dignity soever they be, none be exempted from suffering. Some suffer in body by pains and sickness, some by poverty and want of necessaries, some by loss of friends, some by the disloyalty of those whom they trusted in. Some, again, suffer by loss of their goods by fire, wars, and the like; and some by their own indiscretion, unwariness, and want of foresight, falling into disgrace; some, by setting their affection where it is rejected, grow desperately mad; some thereby living in perpetual discomfort, become woeful murderers of themselves; and some, fortune frowning upon them, have all things go contrary to their desire. In fine, no place, no person, nor any condition can be free from suffering in this miserable life. But shall we think this was ordained by Thee to be thus by chance, or because Thou dost not love what Thou hast made? No! God forbid we should ever think so!

Dame Gertrude More
(1606-1633)

* * *

THIS is my prayer to thee, my lord—strike, strike at the root of penury in my heart.

Give me the strength lightly to bear my joys and sorrows.

Give me the strength to make my love fruitful in service.

Give me the strength never to disown the poor or bend my knees before insolent might.

Give me the strength to raise my mind high above daily trifles.

And give me the strength to surrender my strength to thy will with love.

Rabindranath Tagore
(1861-1941)

* * *

Have mercy
Upon us,
Have mercy
Upon our efforts,
That we
Before Thee,
In love and in faith,
Righteousness and humility,
May follow Thee,
With self-denial, steadfastness, and courage,
And meet Thee
In the silence.

Give us
A pure heart
That we may see Thee,
A humble heart
That we may hear Thee,
A heart of love
That we may serve Thee,
A heart of faith
That we may live Thee,

Thou
Whom I do not know
But Whose I am.

Thou
Whom I do not comprehend
But Who hast dedicated me
To my fate.
Thou—

Dag Hammarskjöld
(1905-1961)

* * *

GRACE BEFORE THE EVENING MEAL

Father, we thank Thee for this day
For food, for fun, for life, for play;
And as the evening shadows fall,
We bring to Thee, dear Lord, our all;
And as we pray, we ask Thy grace
Upon this happy, happy place.
Amen.

William L. Stidger
(1885-1949)

* * *

BLACK ELK'S PRAYER

Grandfather, Great Mysterious One, you have been always, and before you nothing has been.

There is nothing to pray to but you.

The star nations all over the universe are yours, and yours are the grasses of the earth.

Day in, day out, you are the life of things . . .

You are older than all need, older than all pain and prayer.

Grandfather, all over the world the faces of living ones are alike. In tenderness they have come up out of the ground. Look upon your children with children in their arms, that they may face the winds and walk the Good Road to the Day of Quiet.

Teach me to walk the soft earth, a relative to all that live. Sweeten my heart, and fill me with light. Give me the strength to understand and the eyes to see.

Help me, for without you, I am nothing.

Hetchetu aloh!

Adapted by John G. Neihardt
(1881-1973)

* * *

God strengthen me to bear myself,
That heaviest weight of all to bear,
Inalienable weight of care.

All others are outside myself;
I lock the door and bar them out—
The turmoil, tedium, gad-about.

I lock the door upon myself,
And bar them out; but who shall wall
Self from myself, most loathed of all? . . .

God harden me against myself,
This coward with pathetic voice
Who craves for ease, and rest, and joys:

Myself, arch-traitor to myself,
My hollowest friend, my deadliest foe,
My clog whatever road I go.

Yet One there is can curb myself,
Can roll the strangling load from me,
Break off the yoke and set me free.

                              Christina Rossetti
                              (1830-1894)

                        * * *

NEW BETHLEHEM

AGAIN the bright entreating star rebukes
The barren welcome that He came to find
For crowded inn, the heart obsessed by pain,
For stable now, the dark and arrogant mind.

And yet with steadfast joy, foreknowing all
Our long despairs made golden in her son,
Into the mourning city of the soul
Mary expectant brings its promised one.

God speed your hour, Mother of our Hope!
And even in the citadel of pain
Let us behold him—so our doom shall pass
And the great star shall tell of peace again.

Sister Jeremy Finnegan

* * *

HARK, MY SOUL! IT IS THE LORD

Lord, it is my chief complaint
That my love is weak and faint;
Yet I love Thee and adore,
O for grace to love Thee more!

William Cowper
(1731-1800)

* * *

My Jesus, Thou hast toiled and wept enough during
Thy three-and-thirty years on this miserable earth.
Rest Thee, to-day! It is my turn to suffer and to fight.

St. Thérèse of Lisieux
(1873-1897)

* * *

HOLY SONNETS

XXIII

Heare us, O heare us Lord; to thee
A sinner is more musique, when he prayes,
  Than spheares, or Angells praises bee,
In Panegyrique Allelujaes;
      Heare us, for till thou heare us, Lord
      We know not what to say;
Thine eare to our sighes, teares, thoughts gives voice
  and word.
O Thou who Satan heard'st in Job's sicke day.
Heare thy selfe now, for thou in us dost pray.

John Donne
(1571-1631)

* * *

IN HIM WE LIVE

FATHER! I bless thy name that I do live,
And in each motion am made rich with Thee,
That when a glance is all that I can give,
It is a kingdom's wealth, if I but see;
This stately body cannot move, save I
Will to its nobleness my little bring;
My voice its measured cadence will not try,
Save I with every note consent to sing;
I cannot raise my hands to hurt or bless,
But I with every action must conspire
To show me there how little I possess,
And yet that little more than I desire;
May each new act my new allegiance prove,
Till in thy perfect love I ever live and move.

Jones Very
(1813-1880)

* * *

PSALM 130

Out of the depths have I cried unto thee, O Lord.

Lord, hear my voice: let thine ears be attentive to the voice of my supplications.

If thou, Lord, shouldest mark iniquities, O Lord, who shall stand?

But there is forgiveness with thee, that thou mayest be feared.

I wait for the Lord, my soul doth wait, and in his word do I hope.

My soul waiteth for the Lord more than they that watch for the morning: I say, more than they that watch for the morning.

Let Israel hope in the Lord: for with the Lord there is mercy, and with him is plenteous redemption.

And he shall redeem Israel from all his iniquities.

* * *

HUSWIFERY

MAKE me, O Lord, thy Spinning Wheele compleat;
    Thy Holy Worde my Distaff make for mee.
Make mine Affections thy Swift Flyers neate,
    And make my Soule thy holy Spoole to bee.
    My Conversation make to be thy Reele,
    And reele the yarn thereon spun of thy Wheele.

Make me thy Loome then, knit therein this Twine:
    And make thy Holy Spirit, Lord, winde quills:
Then weave the Web thyselfe. The yarn is fine.
    Thine Ordinances make my Fulling Mills.
    Then dy the same in Heavenly Colours Choice,
    All pinkt with Varnish't Flowers of Paradise.

Then cloath therewith mine Understanding, Will,
    Affections, Judgment, Conscience, Memory;
My Words and Actions, that their shine may fill
    My wayes with glory and thee glorify.
    Then mine apparell shall display before yee
    That I am Cloathd in Holy robes for glory.

Edward Taylor
(1642-1729)

* * *

GRACE AFTER MEALS

Blessed be you, O Lord our God, king of the world, who in his goodness feeds the whole wide world.

In grace, in mercy, and in kindness, he gives food to all flesh, for his mercy endures for ever.

And because of his great goodness, we have never lacked food, and may we never suffer want of it, for the sake of his great name.

For he feeds and tends the universe; he does good to the world, and provides food for all the creatures he has wrought.

Blessed be you, O Lord, who feed the universe.

A Jewish Reader
in Time and Eternity

* * *

PRAYER FOR THE NATION

Almighty God, you have given us this good land for our heritage. We humbly ask you that we may always prove ourselves a people mindful of your favor and glad to do your will. Bless our land with honorable endeavor, sound learning and pure manners. Save us from violence, discord and confusion, from pride and arrogance, and from every evil way. Defend our liberties and fashion into one united people the multitude brought here out of many nations and tongues. Endow with the Spirit of wisdom those to whom in your name we entrust the authority of government, that there may be justice and peace at home, and that through obedience to your law we may show forth your praise among the nations on earth. In time of prosperity fill our hearts with thankfulness, and in the day of trouble do not allow our trust in you to fail. We ask all of this through Jesus Christ our Lord. Amen.

Monthly Missalette
November, 1982

* * *

HYMN TO THE NAME OF JESUS

The angels with unwearying voice
  Shall sing Thy praises evermore,
For that Thou didst the world rejoice
  And peace 'twixt God and man restore.

St. Bernard
(1090-1153)

* * *

GENTLE JESUS, MEEK AND MILD

Gentle Jesus, meek and mild,
  Look upon a little child;
Pity my simplicity,
  Suffer me to come to thee.

Charles Wesley
(1707-1788)

* * *

BLESSED BE THE HOLY WILL OF GOD

THE will of God be done by us.
The law of God be kept by us,
Our evil will controlled by us,
Our tongue in check be held by us,
Repentance timely made by us,
Christ's passion understood by us,
Each sinful crime be shunned by us,
Much on the *End* be mused by us,
And Death be blessed found by us,
With Angels' music heard by us,
And God's high praise sung to us,
For ever and for aye.

Anonymous
(Nineteenth Century)

* * *

Jesus, Saviour of human activity to which You have given meaning, Saviour of human suffering to which You have given living value, be also the Saviour of human unity; compel us to discard our pettinesses, and to venture forth, resting upon you, into the undaunted ocean of charity.

Pierre Teilhard de Chardin
(1881-1955)
The Divine Milieu

* * *

My God, I take refuge in thee:

At the sight of thy face all my doubts flee away:
Before I have spoken my grief, thou dost know it:
Wondrous things hast thou done, that I cannot forget:
My grief thou hast banished away, joy abideth for ever:
Thou hast drawn me up by thy hand from the deep dark
    well of illusion:
Heartless I shunned thee, my God, yet thou has re-
    deemed me,
Thou hast brought me back to my Home:

Praise be to thy name,
Joyful praise to thy name!

Nanak
(b. 1469)

* * *

A BETTER RESURRECTION

I have no wit, no words, no tears;
　My heart within me like a stone
Is numbed too much for hopes or fears.
　Look right, look left, I dwell alone;
I lift mine eyes, but dimmed with grief
　No everlasting hills I see;
My life is in the falling leaf:
　O Jesus, quicken me!

My life is like a faded leaf,
　My harvest dwindled to a husk;
Truly my life is void and brief
　And tedious in the barren dusk;
My life is like a frozen thing,
　No bud nor greenness can I see:
Yet rise it shall,—the sap of Spring;
　O Jesus, rise in me!

My life is like a broken bowl,
　A broken bowl that cannot hold
One drop of water for my soul
　Or cordial in the searching cold;
Cast in the fire the perished thing;
　Melt and remould it, till it be
A royal cup for Him, my King:
　O Jesus, drink of me!

Christina Rossetti
(1830-1894)

O God, who hast ordained that whatever is to be desired should be sought by labour, and who, by thy blessing, bringest honest labour to good effect; look with mercy upon my studies and endeavours. Grant me, O Lord, to design only what is lawful and right; and afford me calmness of mind, and steadiness of purpose, that I may so do thy will in this short life, as to obtain happiness in the world to come, for the sake of Jesus Christ our Lord.

Samuel Johnson
(1709-1784)

* * *

Lord, grant me a holy heart,
that sees always what is fine and pure
and is not frightened at the sight of sin,
but creates order wherever it goes.

Grant me a heart that knows nothing of boredom,
of weeping and of sighing.
Let me be not overly concerned with the bothersome
thing I call 'myself.'

Lord, give me a sense of humor
and I will find happiness in life
and profit for others.

St. Thomas More
(1478-1535)

* * *

CORPUS CHRISTI

NOW thou hast come to the end of thy pilgrimage,
  Lord;
Thy lamp glows red like a star at the dim lane's turning:
The bread and the wine of thy supper are set in the
  shadows,
And the gleam of thy cottage calls toilers and
  wanderers home.

In the feathery green of the hedges the chervil is bloom-
  ing—
Petals and wafers of scent, like the Host in a dream. . . .
The night wind is singing the Mass of thy living and
  dying,
O Pilgrim of Love, who at last hast come to thy shrine.

Thou art at peace. At thy journey's end thou sittest,
Thy cheek on thy folded hands, before thee the bread
  and wine,
While far down the sky the yellow moon dips to her
  dying,
And the big stars hang like lamps in the fading west.

Lord of the journey's end, if I too should stumble
At last to the long lane's turning, there may I see
The beckon and gleam of the lamp that is hung in thy
  cottage,
Calling me home to my supper, my friends, and sleep.

The Saints sup with thee, there in the dusk and lamp-
    light—
Mary and Joseph and Peter and all my friends—
With faces propped on their tired and toil-worn fingers,
And kind eyes full of the peace of the journey's end.

To that feast of the Saints in Light, dear Lord, please
    bring me,
Wash my dusty feet as on Maundy long ago;
At the end of the day let me find my Lord at supper,
And forget my toils with him in the Breaking of Bread.

Sheila Kaye-Smith
(1887-1956)

* * *

THE CELESTIAL SURGEON

If I have faltered more or less
In my great task of happiness;
If I have moved among my race
And shown no glorious morning face;
If beams from happy human eyes
Have moved me not; if morning skies,
Books, and my food, and summer rain
Knocked on my sullen heart in vain:—
Lord, thy most pointed pleasure take
And stab my spirit broad awake;
Or, Lord, if too obdurate I,
Choose thou, before that spirit die,
A piercing pain, a killing sin,
And to my dead heart run them in!

Robert Louis Stevenson
(1850-1894)

* * *

PRAYER FOR BROTHERHOOD

O Lord, though we are prone to seek favors for ourselves alone yet when we come into Thy presence, we are lifted above petty thoughts of self. We become ashamed of our littleness and are made to feel that we can worship Thee in holiness only as we serve our brothers in love.

How much we owe to the labors of our brothers! Day by day they dig far away from the sun that we may be warm, enlist in outposts of peril that we may be secure, and brave the terrors of the unknown for truths that shed light on our way. Numberless gifts and blessings have been laid in our cradles as our birthright.

Let us then, O Lord, be just and great-hearted in our dealings with our fellow-men, sharing with them the fruit of our common labor, acknowledging before Thee that we are but stewards of whatever we possess. Help us to be among those who are willing to sacrifice that others may not hunger, who dare to be bearers of light in the dark loneliness of stricken lives, who struggle and even bleed for the triumph of righteousness among men. So may we be co-workers with Thee in the building of Thy kingdom which has been our vision and goal through the ages.

Lewis Browne
(1897-1949)

* * *

TOO LATE

For all the days I've squandered
    In prank and play;
For all the ways I've wandered
    From off Thy way;
For all that doth dissever
    My thought from Thee,
O God of High Endeavour
    Forgive Thou me!

For all the faiths I've fathered
    And counted mine;
For all the gain I've gathered,
    Remote from Thine;
For steps my feet have stumbled,
    Despite Thy Word,
And tasks my hands have fumbled:
    Forgive me Lord!

Now that men soon must grave me,
    And swift the moments haste,
Pardon O Lord, who gave me
    Talents I let to waste!
The man you sought to make me,
    Alas! I now discern . . .
But Oh that it should take me
    All Life to learn!

           Robert Service
           (1874-1958)

* * *

THE ELIXIR

Teach me, my God and King,
    In all things Thee to see;
And what I do in anything,
    To do it as for Thee.

Not rudely, as a beast,
    To run into an actiòn;
But still to make Thee prepossessed,
    And give it his perfectiòn.

A man that looks on glass
    On it may stay his eye,
Or, if he pleaseth, through it pass,
    And then the heaven espy.

All may of Thee partake;
    Nothing can be so mean
Which with his tincture, "for Thy sake,"
    Will not grow bright and clean.

A servant with this clause
    Makes drudgery divine:
Who sweeps a room as for Thy laws
    Makes that and the action fine.

This is the famous stone
    That turneth all to gold;
For that which God doth touch and own
    Cannot for less be told.

George Herbert
(1593-1633)

* * *

ANTHEM

Let us praise our Maker, with true passion extol Him.
Let the whole creation give out another sweetness,
Nicer in our nostrils, a novel fragrance
From cleansed occasions in accord together
As one feeling fabric, all flushed and intact,
Phenomena and numbers announcing in one
Multitudinous oecumenical song
Their grand givenness of gratitude and joy,
Peaceable and plural, their positive truth
An authoritative This, and unthreatened Now
When, in love and in laughter, each lives itself,
For, united by His Word, cognition and power,
System and Order, are a single glory,
And the pattern is complex, their places safe.

W. H. Auden
(1907-1973)

* * *

Lord, it is dark.
Lord, are you here in my darkness?
Where are you, Lord?
Do you love me still?
Or have I wearied you?
Lord, answer,
Answer!

It is dark.

Michel Quoist
(1921-   )

* * *

THE SWEET COMPLAINT
OF THE LOVING MOTHER OF GOD

Most beloved Son,
how could you give such sorrow
to your Mother,
whom you love
and who loves you
so much?

St. Bonaventure
(1221-1274)

* * *

WEARY IN WELL-DOING

I would have gone; God bade me stay:
  I would have worked; God bade me rest.
He broke my will from day to day,
  He read my yearnings unexprest,
    And said them nay.

Now I would stay; God bids me go:
  Now I would rest; God bids me work.
He breaks my heart tost to and fro;
  My soul is wrung with doubts that lurk
    And vex it so.

I go, Lord, where Thou sendest me;
  Day after day I plod and moil:
But, Christ my God, when will it be
  That I may let alone my toil
    And rest with Thee?

Christina Rossetti
(1830-1894)

* * *

THE UNIVERSAL PRAYER
Deo Opt. Max.

Father of All! in every Age,
  In every Clime adored,
By Saint, by Savage, and by Sage,
  Jehovah, Jove, or Lord!

Thou Great First Cause, least understood:
  Who all my Sense confined
To know but this, that Thou art Good,
  And that myself am blind;

Yet gave me, in this dark Estate,
  To see the Good from Ill;
And binding Nature fast in Fate,
  Left free the Human Will.

What Conscience dictates to be done,
  Or warns me not to do,
This, teach me more than Hell to shun,
  That, more than Heaven pursue.

What Blessings thy free Bounty gives,
  Let me not cast away;
For God is payed when Man receives;
  To enjoy is to obey.

Yet not to Earth's contracted Span
  Thy Goodness led me bound,
Or think Thee Lord alone of Man,
  When thousand Worlds are round:

Let not this weak, unknowing hand
  Presume thy bolts to throw,
And deal damnation round the land,
  On each I judge thy Foe.

If I am right, thy grace impart,
  Still in the right to stay;
If I am wrong, oh teach my heart
  To find that better way.

Save me alike from foolish Pride
  Or impious Discontent,
At aught thy Wisdom has denied,
  Or aught thy Goodness lent.

Teach me to feel another's Woe,
  To hide the Fault I see;
That Mercy I to others show,
  That Mercy show to me.

Mean though I am, not wholly so,
  Since quickened by thy Breath;
Oh lead me wheresoe'er I go,
  Through this day's Life or Death.

This day, be Bread and Peace my Lot:
  All else beneath the Sun,
Thou know'st if best bestowed or not;
  And let Thy Will be done.

To thee, whose Temple is all Space,
  Whose Altar Earth, Sea, Skies,
One Chorus let all Being raise,
  All Nature's Incense rise!

Alexander Pope
(1688-1744)

* * *

BITTER-SWEET

Ah my dear angry Lord,
Since thou dost love, yet strike;
Cast down, yet help afford;
Sure I will do the like.
I will complain, yet praise;
I will bewail, approve:
And all my sour-sweet days
I will lament, and love.

George Herbert
(1593-1633)

* * *

THE PURSUIT

LORD! what a busie, restles thing
      Hast thou made man!
Each day and houre he is on wing,
      Rest not a span;
Then having lost the sunne and light,
      By clouds surpriz'd,
He keeps a commerce in the night
      With aire disguis'd;
Hadst thou given to this active dust
      A state untir'd,
The lost sonne had not left the huske
      Nor home desir'd;
That was thy secret, and it is
      Thy mercy too,
For when all failes to bring to blisse,
      Then, this must do.
Ah! Lord! and what a purchase will that
    be,
To take us sick, that sound would not take
    thee?

                Henry Vaughan
                (1622-1695)

* * *

THE PRAYER

Thou knowest, Lord, with what flaming boldness,
my word invokes Thy help for strangers.
I come now to plead for one who was mine,
my cup of freshness, honeycomb of my mouth,
lime of my bones, sweet reason of life's journey,
bird-trill to my ears, girdle of my garment.
Even those who are no part of me are in my care.
Harden not Thine eyes if I plead with Thee for
    this one!

He was a good man, I say he was a man
whose heart was entirely open; a man
gentle in temper, frank as the light of day,
as filled with miracles as the spring of the year.

Thou answerest harshly that he is unworthy of
    entreaty
who did not anoint with prayer his fevered lips,
who went away that evening without waiting for
    Thy sign,
his temples shattered like fragile goblets.

But I, my Lord, protest that I have touched,—
just like the spikenard of his brow,—
his whole gentle and tormented heart:
and it was silky as a nascent bud!

Thou sayest that he was cruel? Thou forgettest,
    Lord, that I loved him,
and that he knew my wounded heart was wholly
    his.

He troubled for ever the waters of my gladness?
It does not matter! Thou knowest: I loved him, I
   loved him!

And to love (Thou knowest it well) is a bitter
   exercise;
a pressing of eyelids wet with tears,
a kissing-alive of hairshirt tresses,
keeping, below them, the ecstatic eyes.

The piercing iron has a welcome chill,
when it opens, like sheaves of grain, the loving
   flesh.
And the cross (Thou rememberest, O King of the
   Jews!)
is softly borne, like a spray of roses.

Here I rest, Lord, my face bowed down
to the dust, talking with Thee through the
   twilight,
through all the twilights that may stretch through
   life,
if Thou art long in telling me the word I await.

I shall weary Thine ears with prayers and sobs;
a timid greyhound, I shall lick Thy mantle's hem.
Thy loving eyes can not escape me,
Thy foot avoid the hot rain of my tears.

Speak at last the word of pardon! It will scatter
in the wind the perfume of a hundred fragrant
   vials

as it empties; all waters will be dazzling;
the wilderness will blossom, the cobblestones will
  sparkle.

The dark eyes of wild beasts will moisten,
and the conscious mountain that Thou didst forge
  from stone
will weep through the white eyelids of its snow-
  drifts;
Thy whole earth will know that Thou hast
  forgiven!

Gabriela Mistral
(1889-1957)

* * *

AN OLD ENGLISH PRAYER

Give us, Lord
a bit of sun
a bit of work and
a bit of fun.
Give us in all the struggle and sputter
Our daily bread and a bit of butter;
Give us health and our keep to make,
And a bit to spare for others' sake;
Give us, too, a bit of song,
And a tale, and a book to help us along.
Give us, Lord, a chance to be
Our goodly best, brave, wise and free,
Our goodly best for ourself and others,
Until all men learn to live as brothers.

* * *

LET only that little be left of me whereby I may name thee my all.

Let only that little be left of my will whereby I may feel thee on every side, and come to thee in everything, and offer to thee my love every moment.

Let only that little be left of me whereby I may never hide thee.

Let only that little of my fetters be left whereby I am bound with thy will, and thy purpose is carried out in my life—and that is the fetter of thy love.

Rabindranath Tagore
(1861-1941)

* * *

CHRIST THE COMRADE

Christ, by Thine own darkened hour
Live within my heart and brain!
Let my hands not slip the rein.

Ah, how long ago it is
Since a comrade rode with me!
Now a moment let me see

Thyself, lonely in the dark,
Perfect, without wound or mark.

Padraic Colum
(1881-1972)

* * *

THE CANTICLE OF BROTHER SUN

Most high omnipotent good Lord,
Yours are the praises, the glory, the honor and all
   blessing.
To you alone, Most High, do they belong,
And no man is worthy to mention you.

Praised be you, my Lord, with all your creatures,
Especially Sir Brother Sun,
Who makes the day and through whom you give us
   light.
And he is beautiful and radiant with great splendor,
And bears the signification of you, Most High One.

Praised be you, my Lord, for Sister Moon and the stars,
You have formed them in heaven clear and precious
   and beautiful.

Praised be you, my Lord, for Brother Wind,
And for the air—cloudy and serene—and every kind of
   weather,
By which you give sustenance to your creatures.

Praised be you, my Lord, for Sister Water,
Which is very useful and humble and precious and
   chaste.

Praised be you, my Lord, for Brother Fire,
By whom you light the night,
And he is beautiful and jocund and robust and strong.

Praised be you, my Lord, for our sister Mother Earth,
Who sustains and governs us,
And produces various fruits with colored flowers and
  herbs.

Praised be you, my Lord, for those who give pardon for
  your love
And bear infirmity and tribulation,
Blessed are those who endure in peace,
For by you, Most High, they will be crowned.

Praised be you, Lord, for our Sister Bodily Death,
From whom no living man can escape.
Woe to those who die in mortal sin.
Blessed are those whom death will find in your most
  holy will,
For the second death shall do them no harm.

Praise and bless my Lord and give him thanks
And serve him with great humility.

St. Francis of Assisi
(c. 1182-1226)

* * *

FOR GRANDPARENTS

For grandmothers and grandfathers,
　praise the Lord.
For the limitless love they share,
　for the concern they show,
　for the prayers they say,
　for the hope they pass on,
　praise the Lord.
For the lines and wrinkles,
　for the limps and liver spots,
　for trifocals and bad knees,
　for gray hair and bald spots,
　praise the Lord.
For the birthdays they never forget,
　for the afghans they knit,
　for the memories they share,
　for the examples they offer,
　praise the Lord.
For the babies they hold,
　for the stories they read,
　for the bragging they do,
　for the pictures they show,
　praise the Lord.
For the day, pray God, when we will be
　grandparents just like them,
　praise the Lord.

　　　　　　　　　Dolores Curran
　　　　　　　　　(1932-　　)

* * *

IN MEMORIAM
A.H.H.
Obiit MDCCCXXXIII

Strong Son of God, immortal Love,
   Whom we, that have not seen thy face,
   By faith, and faith alone, embrace,
Believing where we cannot prove;

Thine are these orbs of light and shade;
   Thou madest Life in man and brute;
   Thou madest Death; and lo, thy foot
Is on the skull which thou has made.

Thou wilt not leave us in the dust:
   Thou madest man, he knows not why;
   He thinks he was not made to die;
And thou hast made him: thou art just.

Thou seemest human and divine,
   The highest,holiest manhood thou:
   Our wills are ours, we know not how;
Our wills are ours, to make them thine.

Our little systems have their day;
   They have their day, and cease to be
   They are but broken lights of thee,
And thou, O Lord, art more than they.

We have but faith: we cannot know;
   For knowledge is of things we see;
   And yet we trust it comes from thee,
A beam in darkness: let it grow.

Let knowledge grow from more to more,
   But more of reverence in us dwell;
   That mind and soul, according well,
May make one music as before,

But vaster. We are fools and slight;
   We mock thee when we do not fear:
   But help thy foolish ones to bear,
Help thy vain worlds to bear thy light.

Forgive what seem'd my sin in me,
   What seem'd my worth since I began;
   For merit lives from man to man,
And not from man, O Lord, to thee.

Forgive my grief for one removed,
   Thy creature, whom I found so fair.
   I trust he lives in thee, and there
I find him worthier to be loved.

Forgive these wild and wandering cries,
   Confusions of a wasted youth;
   Forgive them where they fail in truth,
And in thy wisdom make me wise.

                    Alfred Tennyson
                    (1809-1892)

* * *

O FOR A THOUSAND TONGUES TO SING

O for a thousand tongues to sing
My great Redeemer's praise,
The glories of my God and King,
The triumphs of His grace!

My gracious Master and my God,
Assist me to proclaim,
To spread through all the earth abroad
The honours of Thy name.

Jesus! the name that charms our fears
That bids our sorrows cease;
'Tis music in the sinner's ears,
'Tis life and health and peace.

Charles Wesley
(1707-1788)

* * *

THE DAY'S DEMAND

God give us men! A time like this de-
mands
Strong minds, great hearts, true faith,
and ready hands;
Men whom the lust of office does not
kill;
Men whom the spoils of office cannot
buy;
Men who possess opinions and a will;
Men who have honor; men who will
not lie.

Josiah Gilbert Holland
(1819-1881)

* * *

MORNING AND EVENING HYMN

Praise God, from whom all blessings flow!
Praise Him, all creatures here below!
Praise Him above, ye heavenly host!
Praise Father, Son, and Holy Ghost!

Bishop Thomas Ken
(1637-1711)

* * *

FOR CHRISTIAN UNITY

Lord,
we have been praying
for Christian unity
for so long . . .
Will we ever see it?

You came to achieve unity
so long ago . . .
And what are we doing?

It is still time
to bring this unity about,
provided we understand
that the season of the cross
is not a fruitless one . . .

Draw us together, Lord,
you who ceaselessly reconcile us
with the Father
in the Spirit
for ever and ever.

Pierre Talec
(1933-   )

* * *

Thou who art over us,
Thou who art one of us,
Thou who *art*—
Also within us,
May all see Thee—in me also,
May I prepare the way for Thee,
May I thank Thee for all that shall fall to my lot,
May I also not forget the needs of others,
Keep me in Thy love
As Thou wouldest that all should be kept in mine.
May everything in this my being be directed to Thy glory
And may I never despair.
For I am under Thy hand,
And in Thee is all power and goodness.

Dag Hammarskjöld
(1905-1961)

* * *

HOLY SONNETS

I

Thou hast made me, And shall thy worke decay?
Repaire me now, for now mine end doth haste,
I runne to death, and death meets me as fast,
And all my pleasures are like yesterday;
I dare not move my dimme eyes any way,
Despaire behind, and death before doth cast
Such terrour, and my feeble flesh doth waste
By sinne in it, which it t'wards hell doth weigh;
Only thou art above, and when towards thee
By thy leave I can looke, I rise againe;
But our old subtle foe so tempteth me,
That not one houre my selfe I can sustaine;
Thy Grace may wing me to prevent his art,
And thou like Adamant draw mine iron heart.

John Donne
(1571-1631)

* * *

WEDDING-HYMN, TO _____

Thou God, whose high, eternal Love
  Is the only blue sky of our life,
Clear all the Heaven that bends above
  The life-road of this man and wife.

May these two lives be but one note
  In the world's strange-sounding harmony,
Whose sacred music e'er shall float
  Through every discord up to Thee.

As when from separate stars two beams
  Unite to form one tender ray:
As when two sweet but shadowy dreams
  Explain each other in the day:

So may these two dear hearts one light
  Emit, and each interpret each.
Let an angel come and dwell all night
  In this dear double-heart, and teach!

Sidney Lanier
(1842-1881)

* * *

LUCIS CREATOR OPTIME
(Vespers—Sunday)

FATHER of Lights, by whom each day
   Is kindled out of night,
Who, when the heavens were made, didst lay
   Their rudiments in light;
Thou who didst bind and blend in one
   The glistening morn and evening pale,
Hear Thou our plaint, when light is gone,
   And lawlessness and strife prevail.

Hear, lest the whelming weight of crime
   Wreck us with life in view;
Lest thoughts and schemes of sense and time
   Earn us a sinner's due.
So may we knock at Heaven's door,
   And strive the immortal prize to win,
Continually and evermore
   Guarded without and pure within.

Grant this, O Father, Only Son,
   And Spirit, God of grace,
To whom all worship shall be done
   In every time and place.

John Henry Newman
(1801-1890)

* * *

Thou, O Christ, art all I want,
    More than all in Thee I find!
Raise the fallen, cheer the faint,
    Heal the sick, and lead the blind:
Just and holy is Thy name,
    I am all unrighteousness;
False and full of sin I am,
    Thou art full of truth and grace.

John Wesley
(1703-1791)

* * *

RESIGNATION

Long had I grieved at what I deemed abuse,
But now I am as grain within the mill.
If so be thou must crush me for thy use,
Grind on, O potent God, and do thy will!

Paul Laurence Dunbar
(1872-1906)

* * *

Sweet Lord, what a being is ours? Obliged to reduce
our aim to a simple view of the little part we fill, and in
quiet acceptance insure tranquillity.

St. Elizabeth Seton
(1774-1821)

* * *

PER PACEM AD LUCEM

I do not ask, O Lord, that life may be
    A pleasant road;
I do not ask that Thou wouldst take from me
    Aught of its load;

I do not ask that flowers should always spring
    Beneath my feet;
I know too well the poison and the sting
    Of things too sweet.

For one thing only, Lord, dear Lord, I plead,
    Lead me aright—
Though strength should falter, and though heart should
    bleed—
    Through Peace to Light.

I do not ask, O Lord, that Thou shouldst shed
    Full radiance here;
Give but a ray of peace, that I may tread
    Without a fear.

I do not ask my cross to understand,
    My way to see;
Better in darkness just to feel Thy hand
    And follow Thee.

Joy is like restless day; but peace divine
  Like quiet night:
Lead me, O Lord,—till perfect Day shall shine,
  Through Peace to Light.

Adelaide Anne Procter
(1825-1864)

* * *

PRAYER FOR WINGS

Prostrate, self-scorning,
Wingless and mourning,
Dust in the dust,
We lie as we must:
Empty. To dare not,
Know not and care not
Is our employ.
God, do Thou dower us,
Kindle, empower us,
Give us Thy joy.
Impotence clings—
How shall we bear it?
Wings, give us wings,
Wings of the spirit!

Dmitry Merezhkovsky
(1865-1941)

THREE PRAYERS

I REST with Thee, O Jesus,
And do Thou rest with me.
The oil of Christ on my poor soul,
The creed of the Twelve to make me whole,
Above my head I see.
O Father, who created me,
O Son, who purchased me,
O Spirit Blest, who blessest me,
Rest ye with me.

Great Giver of the open hand.
We stand to thank Thee for our meat.
A hundred praises, Christ, 'tis meet,
For all we drink, for all we eat.

I lie down with God, and may God lie down with me;
The right hand of God under my head,
The two hands of Mary round about me,
The cross of the nine white angels
From the back of my head
To the sole of my feet.
May I not lie with evil,
And may evil not lie with me.

                                        Anonymous

* * *

ABIDE WITH ME

Abide with me: fast falls the eventide;
The darkness deepens; Lord, with me abide:
When other helpers fail, and comforts flee;
Help of the helpless, O abide with me.

Swift to its close ebbs out life's little day;
Earth's joys grow dim, its glories pass away;
Change and decay in all around I see;
O Thou Who changest not, abide with me.

I need Thy presence every passing hour;
What but Thy grace can foil the tempter's power?
Who like Thyself my guide and stay can be?
Through cloud and sunshine, O abide with me.

I fear no foe, with Thee at hand to bless;
Ills have no weight, and tears no bitterness:
Where is death's sting? Where, grave, thy victory?
I triumph still, if Thou abide with me.

Hold Thou Thy cross before my closing eyes;
Shine through the gloom and point me to the skies;
Heaven's morning breaks, and earth's vain shadows
   flee;
In life, in death, O Lord, abide with me.

Henry Francis Lyte
(1793-1847)

* * *

THE PRAYER OF THE OX

Dear God, give me time.
  Men are always so driven!
  Make them understand that I can never hurry.
  Give me time to eat.
  Give me time to plod.
  Give me time to sleep.
  Give me time to think.
           Amen

        Carmen Bernos de Gasztold
        Trans. by Rumer Godden
             (1907-   )

* * *

THE PATER NOSTER OF ST. TERESA

Lord, do not delay. Calm the tumult of this sea, and grant that the Barque of Thy Church may not be tossed about by the tempest. Save us, O Lord, for we perish.

St. Teresa of Avila
(1515-1582)

* * *

i thank you God for most this amazing
day: for the leaping greenly spirits of trees
and a blue true dream of sky; and for everything
which is natural which is infinite which is yes

—e. e. cummings
(1894-1962)

* * *

NOW I AM OLD

Beloved God,
Now I am old,
Help me to be young again,
Help me to seek you
In solid jolly things—
The birds of the air,
The lilies of the field,
A head of counted hair,
A harvest of white grain
Heavy with sunny yield,
A gentle fall of rain,
Things you yourself extolled—
Rather than in abstractions
Like peace and justice and truth
Which man can never bring to birth,
There are too many counter-attractions.
Then, perhaps, I might begin
To be happy again, which is no sin,
For, after all, did you not say
"I come to bring you joy"?

John Griffiths

* * *

O God, who art life, wisdom, truth, bounty and blessedness, the eternal, the only true good, our God and our Lord, who art our hope and our heart's joy: we acknowledge with thanksgiving that thou hast made us in thine Image, and that we may direct our thoughts to thee. Lord, make us to know thee aright, that we may love, enjoy, and possess thee more and more.

St. Anselm
(1033-1109)

* * *

HOPE AND COURAGE

Hope that is seen
is not hope. . . .

We hope for what we do not see,
Help us, Lord, to wait for it
with patience . . .

Father in Heaven,
I know that in everything
you work *for the true good*
of those who love you,
who are called according to your purpose,
whom you desire to be conformed
to the image of your Son
in order that he might be the firstborn
among many brethren . . .

If you, O God, are for us, who is against us?
You did not spare your own Son
but gave him up for us all,
will you not also
give us all things with him?

How secure I am in the love of your Son,
who died, who was raised from the dead,
and who is now at your right hand,
the hand of his Father.
Who shall separate us from the love of Christ?
Shall tribulation,
or distress, or persecution,
or famine, or nakedness,
or peril, or sword? . . .

I am sure
that neither death, nor life,
nor angels, nor principalities,
nor things present, nor things to come,
nor powers,
nor height, nor depth,
nor anything else in all creation,
will be able to separate us
from your love, O God,
in Christ Jesus our Lord.

Saint Paul
Adapted by Paul Hilsdale
(1922-   )

* * *

IF ANY LITTLE WORD OF MINE

If any lift of mine may ease
  The burden of another,
God give me love and care and strength
  To help my ailing brother.

Anonymous
(1880)

* * *

PRAYER FOR AN ORDINARY FAMILY

Thank you, God, for an ordinary family with ordinary problems and joys. We don't seek the model marriage, the brightest children, or the best neighborhood. We are content with the gifts you have sent us—normal children, a good marriage, and satisfying work. For these, we thank you. Let your light shine through our ordinariness.

Dolores Curran
(1932-   )

* * *

This, then, is the ultimate meaning of my daily prayers, this awful waiting. It's not what I feel or think of in them, not the resolutions I make, not any superficial activity of my mind and will that You find pleasing in my prayer. All that is only the fulfillment of a command and, at the same time, the free gift of Your grace. All that is only clearing the ground, so the soul will be ready for that precious moment when You offer it the possibility of losing itself in the finding of You, of praying itself into You.

Give me, O God of my prayer, the grace to continue waiting for You in prayer.

Karl Rahner
(1904-   )

* * *

MASS

What I say I don't feel
What I feel I don't show
What I show isn't real
What is real, Lord—I don't know,
No, no, no—I don't know.

I don't know why every time
I find a new love I wind up destroying it.
I don't know why I'm
So freaky-minded, I keep on kind of enjoying it—
Why I drift off to sleep
With pledges of deep resolve again,
Then along comes the day
And suddenly they dissolve again—
I don't know . . .

What I need I don't have
What I have I don't own
What I own I don't want
What I want, Lord, I don't know.

Leonard Bernstein and Stephen Schwartz
(1918-   )   (1948-   )

* * *

And, finally,
a prayer composed especially for this collection
by Martin E. Marty.

"O Lord God of my salvation . . ." They never told me that this is how things would be. They—was it parents or priests?—let me think that there would be joy *or* sorrow, joy in You *or* sorrow in the world or myself. That is not how it turned out.

Sometimes, as during this prayer, I am in the range of joy. I can psalm a line to You, the source of all, and thus the source of joy. Then comes the stab: is there any One to respond? Does my prayer reach the ceiling, the curve of the sky, the bottom of my own heart, and echo back only to my own ears? With the question comes new sorrow.

Sorrow: he (she) whom I loved is absent, alien, dead— it makes little difference which. Dreams die. That undertone of trust which the child in me thought I would always carry now hardly sounds. Did anything add up to anything? Will it? Worst of all: am I on the verge of self-pity, and thus beyond reach of the grand Joy or Sorrow?

Joy: I reach for the Psalms, for the eighty-eighth, to help find a voice beyond my own. Someone else has been where I am, has gone further. "I am counted with

them that go down into the pit . . . Shall thy loving kindness be declared in the grave? or thy faithfulness in
destruction? . . . Thy terrors have cut me off . . . Lover
and friend hast thou put far from me, and mine
acquaintance into darkness."

That's a *Psalm,* a song to You? I find no affirmation
beyond the first line, "O Lord God of my salvation . . ."
Nothing more. Only that reaching out, in a cry. Only
that reaching. And, yet, it is enough, or begins to be
enough. If the cry is to be uttered from pit and grave
and destruction, if it is uttered, I *have* affirmed. Then
there is so little more that I need ask. Strength for this
day. The gift to say a firmer "Yes" if something bids
for a stronger sign. The warmth in half-smiles from
half-strangers as signals of what can come. My call to
support another and grow in strength for the exercise.
Hope for tomorrow.

The shadows of the pit remain, yet I can still cry, "O
Lord God of my salvation." Today, that is enough. I can
even hint: Amen.

Martin E. Marty
(1928-   )

* * *